The Sailor's Little Book

PEYTON

The Sailor's Little Book

Sayings of the Sea

COMPILED BY
BASIL MOSENTHAL

Copyright © Basil Mosenthal 2000

First published 2000 by Fernhurst Books
Duke's Path, High Street, Arundel, West Sussex BN18 9AJ, UK
Tel: 01903 882277 Fax: 01903 882715
Email: sales@fernhurstbooks.co.uk
Website: www.fernhurstbooks.co.uk

Contact the publisher for a free, full-colour brochure.

British Library cataloguing in Publication data: A catalogue record for this book
is available from the British Library.

ISBN 1-898660-76-X
Printed and bound in Singapore

INTRODUCTION

This little book is a nautical jumble
of 'sea wisdom' for present day sailors,
combined with quotations and all sorts
of items about sailors and the sea.
Some are serious, some are humorous;
all make good bunkside (or bedside) reading,
both for sailors and landlubbers.

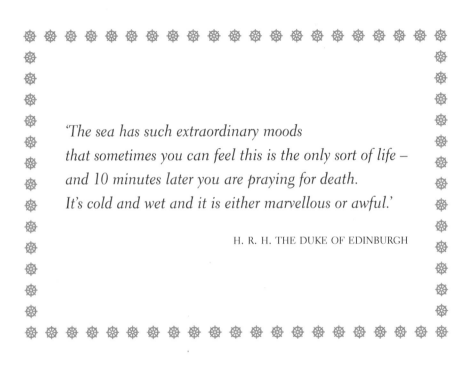

'The sea has such extraordinary moods
that sometimes you can feel this is the only sort of life –
and 10 minutes later you are praying for death.
It's cold and wet and it is either marvellous or awful.'

H. R. H. THE DUKE OF EDINBURGH

Warming the bell is a sailor's expression
for doing something early or ahead of time.
In earlier days the neck of an hourglass
could – at least, in theory – be warmed
to make the sand run through more quickly.

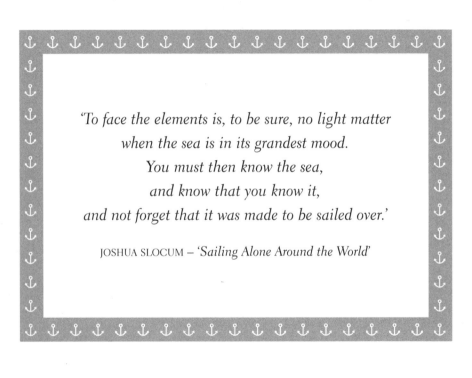

'To face the elements is, to be sure, no light matter
when the sea is in its grandest mood.
You must then know the sea,
and know that you know it,
and not forget that it was made to be sailed over.'

JOSHUA SLOCUM – 'Sailing Alone Around the World'

Even as late as 1965 the official Beaufort Scale not only showed the likely sea state alongside the wind strength, but also a *Coastal Criterion* which was evidently advice for fishing vessels. For instance:

Force 4 – *Moderate breeze – Good working breeze –* Smacks carrying all sail heel over considerably.

Force 7 – *Near Gale* – Smacks remain in harbour and those at sea lie to.

And you could be sure that alongside **Force 10**, some wag would have written 'Smacks on the bottom'.

Weather Lore – Old but True!

A red sky at night is a sailor's delight
A red sky in the morning is a sailorman's warning.

Mackerel sky and mare's tails
Make lofty ships carry low sails.

When the wind shifts against the sun,
Trust it not, for back it will run.

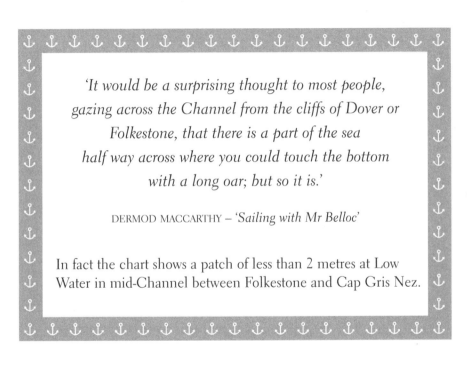

*'It would be a surprising thought to most people,
gazing across the Channel from the cliffs of Dover or
Folkestone, that there is a part of the sea
half way across where you could touch the bottom
with a long oar; but so it is.'*

DERMOD MACCARTHY – *'Sailing with Mr Belloc'*

In fact the chart shows a patch of less than 2 metres at Low
Water in mid-Channel between Folkestone and Cap Gris Nez.

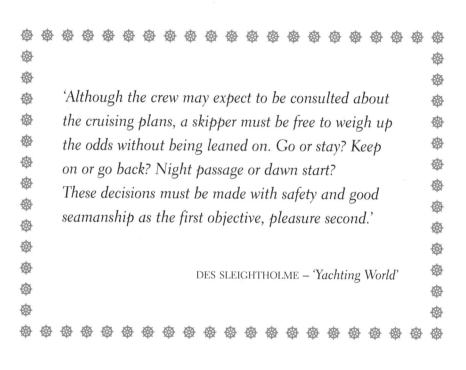

'Although the crew may expect to be consulted about the cruising plans, a skipper must be free to weigh up the odds without being leaned on. Go or stay? Keep on or go back? Night passage or dawn start? These decisions must be made with safety and good seamanship as the first objective, pleasure second.'

DES SLEIGHTHOLME – 'Yachting World'

The traditional leadline had a definite system of marks. For instance:

2 fathoms – two strips of leather
5 fathoms – a piece of white duck
10 fathoms – leather with a hole in it
and so on.

So a good leadsman could not only see the marks by day, but recognize them in the dark by their feel.

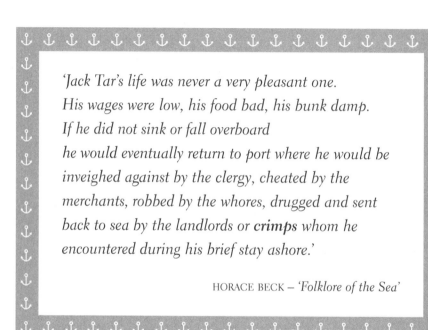

'Jack Tar's life was never a very pleasant one.
His wages were low, his food bad, his bunk damp.
If he did not sink or fall overboard
he would eventually return to port where he would be
inveighed against by the clergy, cheated by the
merchants, robbed by the whores, drugged and sent
back to sea by the landlords or **crimps** whom he
encountered during his brief stay ashore.'

HORACE BECK – 'Folklore of the Sea'

In the early part of WW II, Wrens were trying to buy available stocks of Navy serge to make trousers. It is said that a C-in-C made the following signal:

'Wrens clothing is to be held up until the needs of seagoing personnel have been satisfied.'

Not so long ago, near Piraeus in Greece, a large sailing yacht was being launched after a refit in a shipyard where things had not changed much over the centuries. But the cradle stuck half way into the water. Eventually (because nothing was being hurried) the yacht's skipper was informed that the yard had sent for a tug – and a priest.

The outcome was successful, and the yard blamed themselves for not having had the new cradle blessed before it was used.

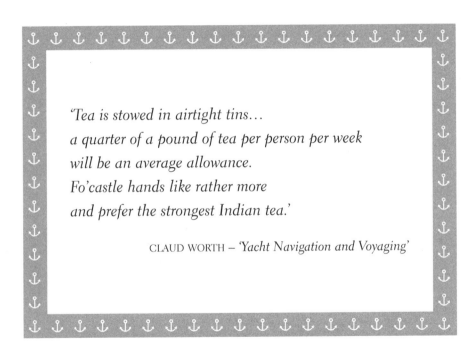

'Tea is stowed in airtight tins…
a quarter of a pound of tea per person per week
will be an average allowance.
Fo'castle hands like rather more
and prefer the strongest Indian tea.'

CLAUD WORTH – 'Yacht Navigation and Voyaging'

'Many things which seem to be risks are risks no longer
if that risk has been gauged beforehand
to a nicety and countered.'

JOHN IRVING – *'The Yachtsman's Weekend Book'*

'One hand for the ship and one for yourself.'

A very old saying that still makes complete sense.

'There is nothing – absolutely nothing –
half so much worth doing
as simply messing about in boats.'

KENNETH GRAHAME – *'The Wind in the Willows'*

The best loved of all quotations for sailors?

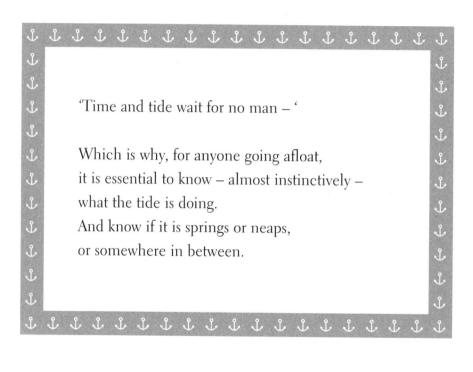

'Time and tide wait for no man – '

Which is why, for anyone going afloat,
it is essential to know – almost instinctively –
what the tide is doing.
And know if it is springs or neaps,
or somewhere in between.

Harbours are not always completely safe places. People fall overboard in harbour more often than at sea. And there are more accidents in dinghies than in yachts, often through overloading, and often at night. Which is when most drinking occurs…

'Good reliable radio contact
with the Rescue Services
should not be seen as an excuse
for a sloppily prepared boat,
on the grounds that:

"if I get into trouble, I can ask for help".'

ROYAL YACHTING ASSOCIATION

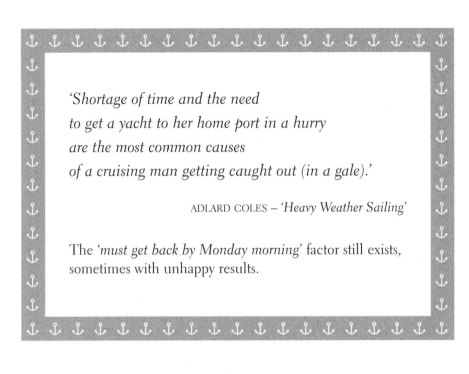

'Shortage of time and the need
to get a yacht to her home port in a hurry
are the most common causes
of a cruising man getting caught out (in a gale).'

ADLARD COLES – *'Heavy Weather Sailing'*

The *'must get back by Monday morning'* factor still exists,
sometimes with unhappy results.

If you watch yachts berthing alongside, it is surprising how often someone makes a mess of throwing a line ashore. A line cannot be thrown properly unless it is properly coiled to start with, and so it starts with knowing how to coil a line.

For some, 'A place for everything, and everything in its place' may sound like fussy and boring advice! But it really is essential in a boat.

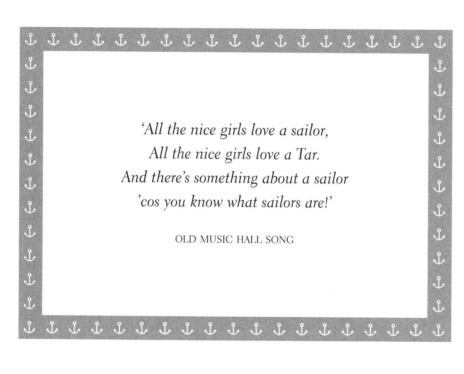

'All the nice girls love a sailor,
All the nice girls love a Tar.
And there's something about a sailor
'cos you know what sailors are!'

OLD MUSIC HALL SONG

Two Thoughts for the Day

The most effective bilge pump
is a frightened man with a bucket.

A good knot should never come undone on its
own, but be easy to untie.

'In today's comfortable navigation stations,
bristling with toys, there is even more temptation
to sit below watching them than there was
in the good old days of pencil and plotter.
But resist them like the jades they are.
Look outside where the action is.
The rocks, the boats, and the squalls are all there
in a richer, more colourful world.'

TOM CUNLIFFE – *'Yachting Monthly'*

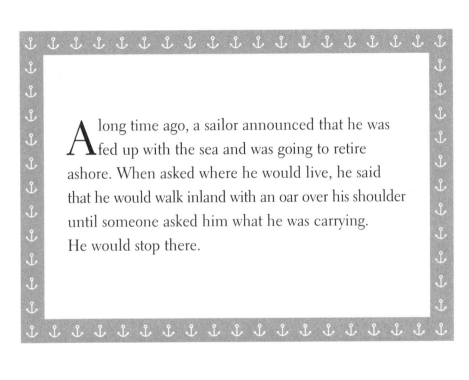

A long time ago, a sailor announced that he was fed up with the sea and was going to retire ashore. When asked where he would live, he said that he would walk inland with an oar over his shoulder until someone asked him what he was carrying. He would stop there.

'The safety of a yacht ultimately depends mainly on the crew. If they are not functioning efficiently because of physical deficiency – be it lack of sleep, proper meals, or cold, then survival is in question. Basic seamanship demands that this does not happen.'

From ROYAL OCEAN RACING CLUB *Special Regulations*

This may sound very earnest,
but it could equally apply to a cruising yacht.

After a day's racing during Cowes Week, yacht crews regularly carouse in the beer tents and pubs ashore. So spare a thought for the sailing ship crews of the last century spending their first night ashore after anything up to a hundred and fifty days at sea. No wonder they found the dubious shoreside joys of the seaports so attractive.

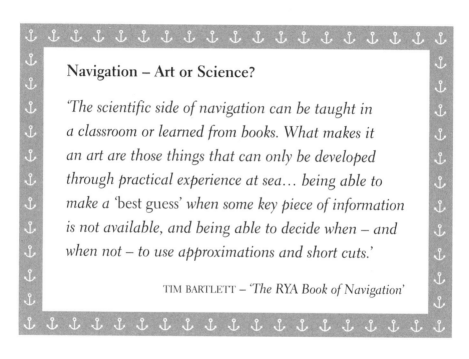

Navigation – Art or Science?

'The scientific side of navigation can be taught in a classroom or learned from books. What makes it an art are those things that can only be developed through practical experience at sea... being able to make a 'best guess' when some key piece of information is not available, and being able to decide when – and when not – to use approximations and short cuts.'

TIM BARTLETT – 'The RYA Book of Navigation'

Sailing close to the wind is a proper and seamanlike activity and can be a skilled one. So it seems a bit unfair that ashore, anyone said to be *sailing close to the wind* is keeping just within the law.

Money for old rope – meaning easy money. In sailing ship days some crews were allowed to unpick lengths of old unneeded rope and sell it ashore for use as caulking.

Show a leg! may be the traditional encouragement for a sailor to wake up. But it originated from the old days of sail when women were allowed to spend a night on board, and a hairless female leg thrust out of a hammock entitled the owner to an extra hour's lie-in.

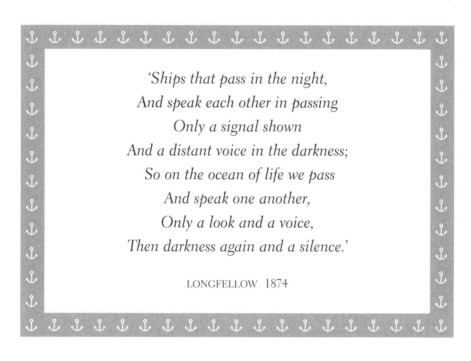

'Ships that pass in the night,
And speak each other in passing
Only a signal shown
And a distant voice in the darkness;
So on the ocean of life we pass
And speak one another,
Only a look and a voice,
Then darkness again and a silence.'

LONGFELLOW 1874

What has Beethoven's Moonlight Sonata got to do with the sea? Not much, except a wartime memory of a completely fascinated audience of minesweeper crews listening to it being played – by moonlight – in Capri (of all places).

Effective astro navigation was not possible until the invention of the first reliable seagoing chronometer by Harrison (of *Longitude* fame) in 1736. And until recently a ship's chronometer was an expensive and cossetted piece of equipment. But the invention of quartz watches and almost universal radio time signals means that a very modest watch can be almost as accurate as an expensive chronometer.

Cockpit, as we now know it in a yacht, seems to derive from the pit where cock fighting took place. In fact the first use of cockpit at sea was in the old sailing navies and was the area below decks where, in battle, the surgeon performed his grisly task. Lord Nelson died down below in the *Victory's* cockpit.

A group of skippers were asked what they thought were the most useful tools on board. Several included a really sharp knife, which – surprisingly – is not always available. Some skippers also listed a serrated bread knife, which can be effective for cutting many things other than bread.

On the Quay 1770

'Who are you, my little man, sitting woebegone and wan,
With your little bundle by your side, waiting for the tide?
You are very small to go to sea,
And I wonder what your fate will be;
Fever, or shot, or Captain's sword,
Or – "Midshipman overboard!"
But don't be doleful. Lift up your head.
Here's an apple for you, and some gingerbread
Now, boy, who did you say you were? "Horatio Nelson, sir".'

DOROTHY MARGARET STUART

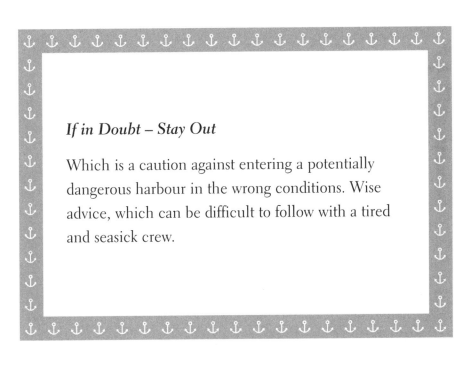

If in Doubt – Stay Out

Which is a caution against entering a potentially
dangerous harbour in the wrong conditions. Wise
advice, which can be difficult to follow with a tired
and seasick crew.

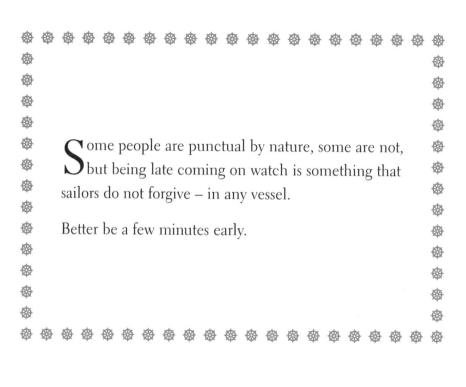

Some people are punctual by nature, some are not, but being late coming on watch is something that sailors do not forgive – in any vessel.

Better be a few minutes early.

By Guess and by God

A pre-GPS form of navigation whereby the skipper relies on experience, instinct, memory and implicit faith rather than on more orthodox methods.

Some sailors still think that it has its merits.

A lifeboat was called out to a yacht in trouble in dirty weather. The coastguard, trying to confirm the yacht's exact position, called it on the radio:

'What is your position?

Repeat, What is your position?'

The skipper came back with his answer:

'My position?... well, I am the marketing director of a computer software firm in the Midlands...'

'It is not generally realised that size is no real criterion of the seaworthiness of a vessel. A corked bottle is quite a fragile thing, but it will survive the worst hurricane that ever blew.'

HUMPHREY BARTON – 'Atlantic Adventures in Small Craft'

'Ships are all right – it's the men in them.'

JOSEPH CONRAD

On the pre-war China Station, when Navy ships had no laundries, an earnest Flag Lieutenant was concerned about his Admiral's washing and sent this signal to the Port Captain:

'Please send Admiral's woman on board.'

Understandably this caused some consternation ashore and the signal was queried. A hurried correction was sent from the flagship:

'Reference my signal please insert washer between Admiral and woman.'

The Coastguard records generally show that more small craft need assistance because of engine breakdowns than for any other reason. And often it may just be running out of fuel. Nowadays a wise yacht skipper, even though he may not approve of the modern reliance on engines, tries not only to be a good seaman and navigator, but a useful mechanic as well.

To Sail or Not to Sail?

'Don't be deterred by the wind in the harbour.
It is seldom as bad outside as it sounds inside.
At least go out and look at it.'

JOHN IRVING – 'The Yachtsman's Weekend Book'

'A young man was being interviewed about his suitability to join the Royal Marine Commando's. Asked if he had previous work experience that might be useful, he replied:
"Well, I did once have a job in an abbatoir".'

PAT MCLAREN – 'Hearts of Oak'

Overheard by the Coastguard when dealing with a distress call from a yacht – the irate voice of the skipper's wife in the background talking to the skipper: *'You got me into this mess and you can jolly well get me out of it.'*

Plan any passage, long or short, with consideration of the weather and of the crew's strength and ability. A trip that a strong crew can take in their stride can be too much for an inexperienced crew. Tiredness and seasickness can soon bring on an inability to cope. Ask any lifeboat coxwain.

'I would rather die of thirst, ten miles off the headlands in a brazen calm, having lost my dinghy in the previous storm, than have on board what today is monstrously called an auxiliary.'

HILAIRE BELLOC.

This should be taken as the remarks of a much revered literary eccentric rather then advice to the modern yachtsman!

It has been said that 'anyone who has the mathematical ability to add up the houshold accounts can navigate'. But does the reverse apply?

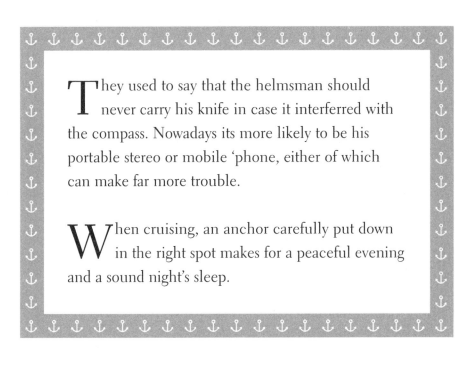

They used to say that the helmsman should never carry his knife in case it interferred with the compass. Nowadays its more likely to be his portable stereo or mobile 'phone, either of which can make far more trouble.

When cruising, an anchor carefully put down in the right spot makes for a peaceful evening and a sound night's sleep.

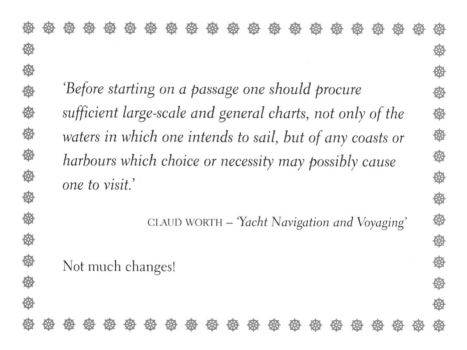

'Before starting on a passage one should procure sufficient large-scale and general charts, not only of the waters in which one intends to sail, but of any coasts or harbours which choice or necessity may possibly cause one to visit.'

CLAUD WORTH – 'Yacht Navigation and Voyaging'

Not much changes!

'When a yacht is running before the wind, it always makes sense to rig a preventer to keep the mainsail under control.
If the wind is right aft it is essential to do so.
Good helming will reduce the need for a preventer,
but a preventer will not reduce the need for good helming.'

'Yachting Monthly'

[A preventer is a rope to hold out the boom.]

'And then we began "to take it off her", to snug her down. We went up to the clewlines and clewed the royals up. Then it was "Up there you boys and make the royals fast". My royal was the mizzen-royal, a rag of a sail among the clouds, which was leaping and slatting a hundred and sixty feet above me. The wind beat me down against the shrouds, it banged me and beat me, and blew the tears from my eyes. In the crosstrees I learned what wind was.'

JOHN MASEFIELD – 'A Tarpaulin Muster'

Maybe a bit humbling when one is winding in a few turns to 'snug down' the self-furling jib.

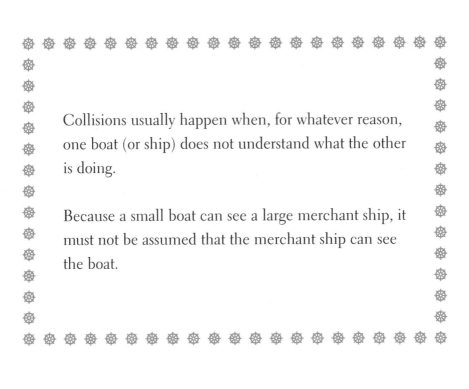

Collisions usually happen when, for whatever reason, one boat (or ship) does not understand what the other is doing.

Because a small boat can see a large merchant ship, it must not be assumed that the merchant ship can see the boat.

'He who sails through the crowd of boats that collect on a public holiday must bear in mind that numbers of those who are in charge of these craft have no experience whatever of watermanship, and are wholly ignorant of the Rules of the Road.'

E. F .KNIGHT – *'Small Boat Handling'*

Things may not have changed entirely in 99 years.

A delivery skipper was asked to sail a boat away from a European country where new tax laws were making things hard for yacht owners. The boat's owner told him that he would have no trouble in getting clearance because the boat was flying the Blue Ensign. The skipper replied: 'Yes, maybe. But it might be easier if the ensign were flying the right way up.'

A yachtsman may look confidently at the latitude and longitude showing on his GPS screen. But it may not mean that he knows where he is on the chart. A position is better plotted on a chart rather than represented by figures on a dial. Especially if the power fails and the numbers are forgotten.

It is a seagoing tradition, (by no means always observed), that a sailor, returning from a cheerful evening ashore, should not disturb his messmates.

Nowadays one might add:
'nor everyone else in the marina or in the anchorage.'

An anchor is not only for tethering a boat to the ground overnight, it can be her brakes in an emergency – such as when the engine fails in a tideway or a busy harbour. And the crew should always know how to apply the brakes in a hurry.

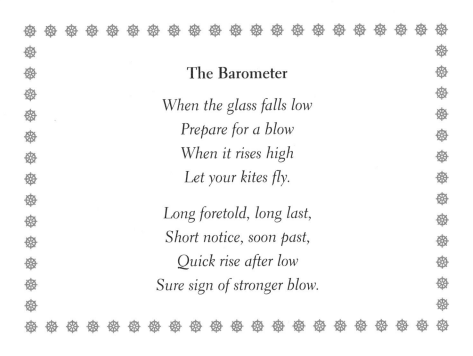

The Barometer

When the glass falls low
Prepare for a blow
When it rises high
Let your kites fly.

Long foretold, long last,
Short notice, soon past,
Quick rise after low
Sure sign of stronger blow.

Entering a new harbour for the first time can be a highly enjoyable part of cruising. But whether it is up a straightforward buoyed channel or an interesting meander between the sandbanks, the wise skipper will have done some homework beforehand.

Finding your way into a strange harbour off the cuff is not recommended.

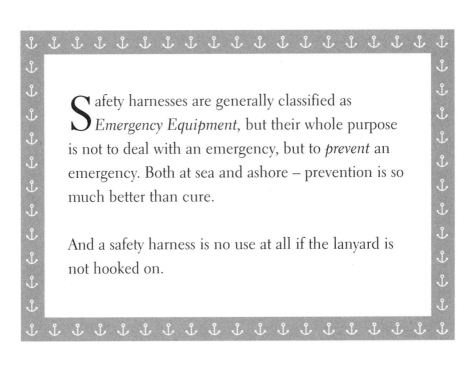

Safety harnesses are generally classified as *Emergency Equipment*, but their whole purpose is not to deal with an emergency, but to *prevent* an emergency. Both at sea and ashore – prevention is so much better than cure.

And a safety harness is no use at all if the lanyard is not hooked on.

*'That couldn't happen to me –
I wouldn't be such an idiot.'*
or
'There, but for the grace of God, go I.'

The reports of rescues at sea – dramatic or routine,
windsurfers or yachts – are always worth thinking
about. Why was the rescue needed?
The idea that accidents only happen to other people
is a dangerous one – both afloat and ashore.

Keeping a good lookout. Usually infers looking earnestly ahead. But it should also mean looking astern as well. Merchant ships can close on you very quickly these days.

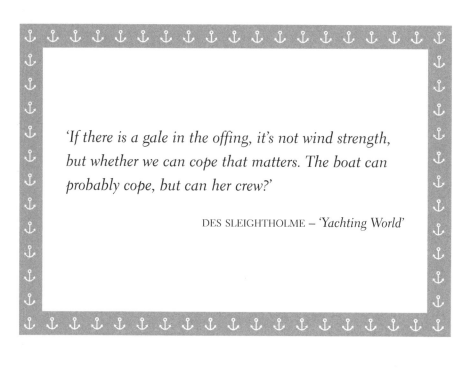

'If there is a gale in the offing, it's not wind strength, but whether we can cope that matters. The boat can probably cope, but can her crew?'

DES SLEIGHTHOLME – 'Yachting World'

In the fifties the destroyer HMS *Comus* was stationed in the Far East. The ship's official motto was *'Lead on apace'*, which is a quotation from Milton's *'Comus'*.

However, during visits to such places as Hong Kong, Singapore, and ports in Japan, where the runs ashore were (to say the least) lively, the unofficial motto became: *'What hath night to do with sleep?'*

– which is also a quotation from Milton.

Keeping a weather eye open.

Said to originate from keeping an eye open to windward where the first signs of any change in the weather might be expected.

But now accepted as referring to a good sailor's instinctive awareness of the weather and what it might do, even though he may have the latest forecast.

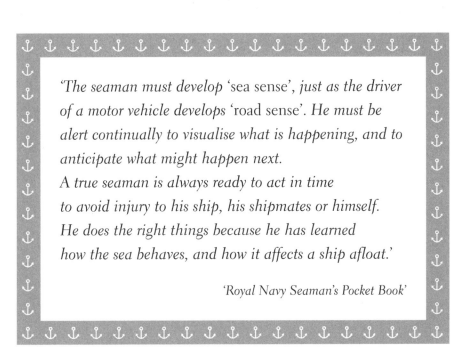

'The seaman must develop 'sea sense', just as the driver of a motor vehicle develops 'road sense'. He must be alert continually to visualise what is happening, and to anticipate what might happen next.

A true seaman is always ready to act in time to avoid injury to his ship, his shipmates or himself.

He does the right things because he has learned how the sea behaves, and how it affects a ship afloat.'

'Royal Navy Seaman's Pocket Book'

As any good engineer will hasten to tell you, engine compartments and engine rooms are not naturally dirty places, and a clean engine makes it much easier to spot oil or water leaks and other defects.

'Ships are but boards, sailors are but men.'

WILLIAM SHAKESPEARE – *'The Merchant of Venice'*

Was this Shakespeare's way of saying that the essence of a ship is those who sail her?

A good crew have been known to nurse a leaking hull safely into harbour.

A sound and well equipped vessel can come to grief with a poor crew.

'Two white lights and and a green one above may look like a fishing vessel to you, and from where you are this makes good sense. But the experienced 'Yottigator' toys with the idea that this could also be a frontal view of Broadstairs High Street.'

BILL LUCAS AND ANDREW SPEDDING – 'Sod's Law of the Sea'

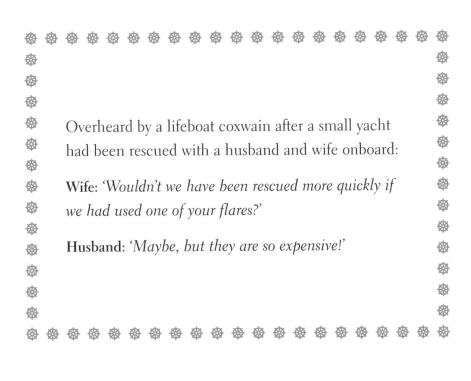

Overheard by a lifeboat coxwain after a small yacht had been rescued with a husband and wife onboard:

Wife: *'Wouldn't we have been rescued more quickly if we had used one of your flares?'*

Husband: *'Maybe, but they are so expensive!'*

The sea is often said to be unforgiving. But it can be remarkably tolerant of fools – until it finally gets bored with them and has its way.

'But amid all the diversity of buttons and keys to be pressed, one was missing, labelled 'wisdom and common sense', the human factor we ignore at our peril.'

DES SLEIGHTHOLME – *'Yachting World'*

Among the countless unfortunates who have been shipwrecked over the ages was *Admiral Sir Clowdisley Shovel*, a distinguished naval officer who went to sea at the age of twelve. However in 1707 he managed to wreck his own warship, and three others, on the Scillies in a storm. Being a very fat man, he floated ashore but was murdered on the beach by a local woman for the conspicuous emerald ring he was wearing. Later this ring was recovered and returned to his heirs, while he was duly buried in Westminster Abbey.

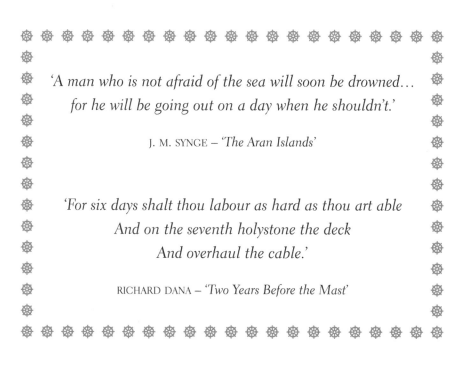

'A man who is not afraid of the sea will soon be drowned...
for he will be going out on a day when he shouldn't.'

J. M. SYNGE – 'The Aran Islands'

'For six days shalt thou labour as hard as thou art able
And on the seventh holystone the deck
And overhaul the cable.'

RICHARD DANA – 'Two Years Before the Mast'

Some navigation exams require an ability to make very precise tidal calculations to within fractions of a meter. This is fine if you are concerned about passing under a bridge or planning to dry out alongside.

But in the open sea, say crossing a bar or passing over a sandbank, you would be very unwise to allow such a small margin for error unless it was flat calm and you knew exactly where you were and what you were doing.

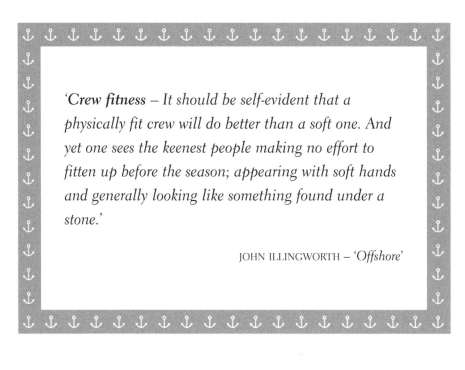

'**Crew fitness** – It should be self-evident that a physically fit crew will do better than a soft one. And yet one sees the keenest people making no effort to fitten up before the season; appearing with soft hands and generally looking like something found under a stone.'

JOHN ILLINGWORTH – '*Offshore*'

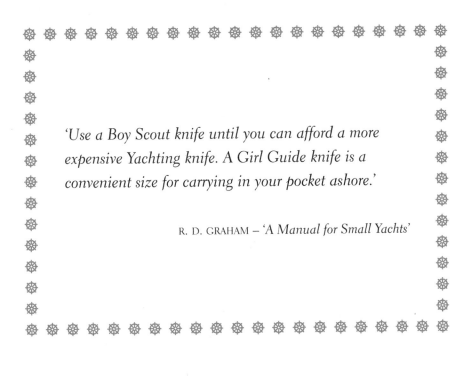

'Use a Boy Scout knife until you can afford a more expensive Yachting knife. A Girl Guide knife is a convenient size for carrying in your pocket ashore.'

R. D. GRAHAM – 'A Manual for Small Yachts'

Ropes, which started off thousands of years ago as plaited reeds, have been in use ever since man went afloat. They were first used with primitive stone anchors.

But a super-tanker still needs ropes to secure itself alongside, and obviously ropes remain an essential part of any modern sailing vessel. So, knowing how to handle them, and tie a few simple knots is an integral part of a sailor's know-how, and always likely to remain so.

The Royal Navy firmly insists that shoes laces are *tied*, and that ships are *secured* alongside.

The traditional definition of a 'prime seaman' was a man who could 'hand, reef, and steer'. 'Hand', less used nowadays, refers to furling a sail. So, all in all, the definition still generally applies in a yacht today.

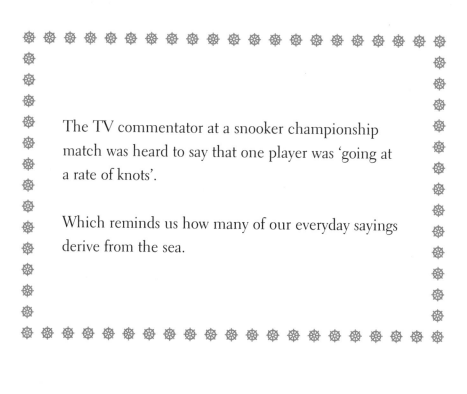

The TV commentator at a snooker championship match was heard to say that one player was 'going at a rate of knots'.

Which reminds us how many of our everyday sayings derive from the sea.

'Lubber'. The sailor's name for a clumsy seaman, hence 'land-lubber'.

But why the 'lubber's line', which is an essential part of a steering compass? There would not seem to be anything especially *lubberly* in using it.

No doubt there is an answer.

On almost every marina, dock, or slipway – in any country – there will be someone ready to give you advice (often incorrect) about berthing your boat, the weather, the tide, and almost any other marine subject.

But, even in these enlightened days, that someone never seems to be female.

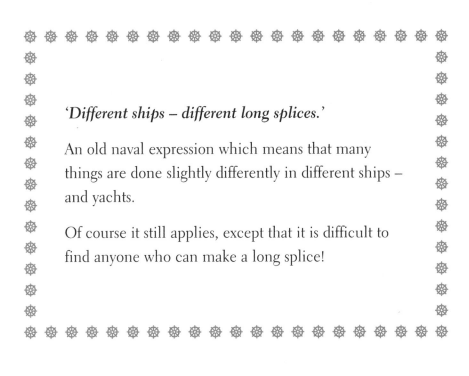

'Different ships – different long splices.'

An old naval expression which means that many
things are done slightly differently in different ships –
and yachts.

Of course it still applies, except that it is difficult to
find anyone who can make a long splice!

Old Navy Food!

Nuts and bolts with an awning – steak and kidney pie
Spithead pheasant – a kipper
Kye or *Ky* – cocoa
Train smash – bacon and tinned tomatoes
Tiddy oggy – Cornish pasty

and the *Custard Bosun* was the Chief cook.

Pusser's kye or cocoa used to be made with Navy issue solid unsweetened chocolate, crumbled up and mixed with plenty of tinned milk and sugar until it was the consistency of pea soup. It was *the* hot drink for a wet, cold, night watch, (especially if accompanied by a 'corned dog' sandwich).

But, like many good things, it has been modernised.

There is a profound difference between time and tide's attendance upon man. Sooner or later the tide always turns.

'Dawn off the Foreland – the young flood making.'

RUDYARD KIPLING – *'Minesweepers'*

Splendid poetry and old fashioned, but evocative sailor's language.

Soldier's wind. Used to be the unflattering term for a wind coming from the beam, which makes for the easiest sailing. In fairness, it derives from the same era between the two wars when it was said that:

'The three most useless things in a yacht are a step ladder, a wheelbarrow, and a naval officer.'

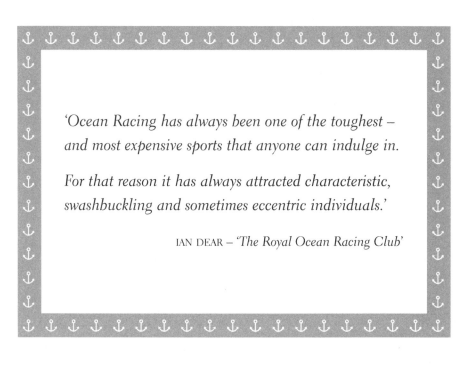

*'Ocean Racing has always been one of the toughest –
and most expensive sports that anyone can indulge in.*

*For that reason it has always attracted characteristic,
swashbuckling and sometimes eccentric individuals.'*

IAN DEAR – *'The Royal Ocean Racing Club'*

It used to be said that owning and sailing an ocean racer is like standing under a cold shower and tearing up five pound notes.

That still may apply – except that the notes will be of a larger denomination!

'Let us think of them that sleep, full many a fathom deep.'

THOMAS CAMPBELL, 1805

The fathom, an English gift to the maritime world, has disappeared from our charts, and is not so much used now. It is based on an old English word meaning *to embrace*, and is the measurement of the outstretched arms of the average man – six feet.

And, of course, 'to fathom out' means *to get to the bottom of,* or *thoroughly understand.*

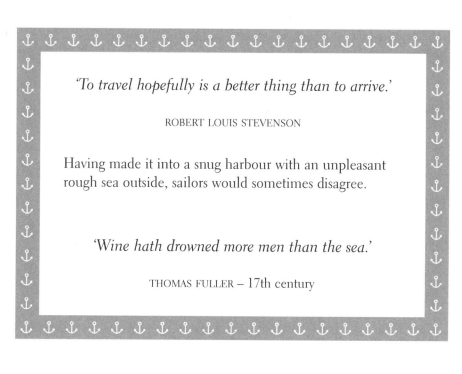

'To travel hopefully is a better thing than to arrive.'

ROBERT LOUIS STEVENSON

Having made it into a snug harbour with an unpleasant rough sea outside, sailors would sometimes disagree.

'Wine hath drowned more men than the sea.'

THOMAS FULLER – 17th century

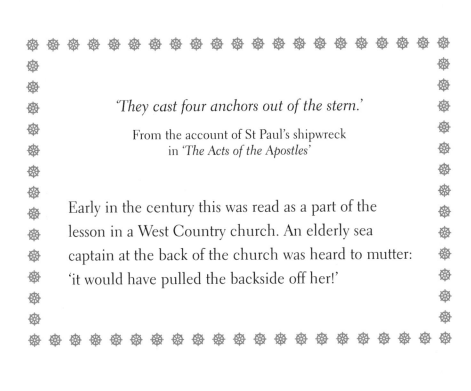

'They cast four anchors out of the stern.'

From the account of St Paul's shipwreck
in *'The Acts of the Apostles'*

Early in the century this was read as a part of the
lesson in a West Country church. An elderly sea
captain at the back of the church was heard to mutter:
'it would have pulled the backside off her!'

Originally a 'chandler' was someone who sold candles.

Signal from Destroyer to unknown Trawler:
'What is the significance of the signal you are flying?'
Reply from Trawler:
'Regret I do not know. Flags smelt of fish.'

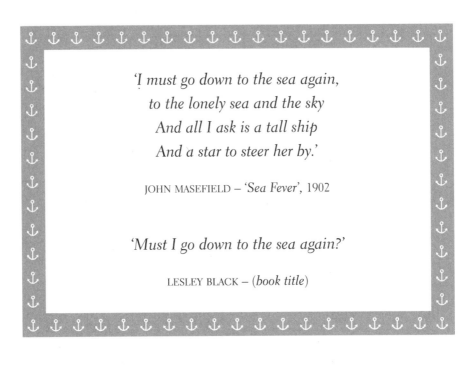

'I must go down to the sea again,
to the lonely sea and the sky
And all I ask is a tall ship
And a star to steer her by.'

JOHN MASEFIELD – 'Sea Fever', 1902

'Must I go down to the sea again?'

LESLEY BLACK – (book title)

Traditionally, scruffy rope ends were the sign of a carelessly run ship. They still are.

When *essential things to carry on board* are discussed, the humble wire coathanger may not be in the list – but everyone will agree how often it has been useful, and sometimes quite essential.

'The chart will tell what the North Atlantic looks like. But what the chart will not tell you is the strength and fury of that ocean, its moods, its violence, its gentle balm, its treachery: what man can do with it, and what it can do with men.'

NICHOLAS MONSARRAT – *'The Cruel Sea'*

For many sailors the over-riding memory of the North Atlantic is greyness – grey skies, grey seas, and, perhaps, loneliness.

Was this the inspiration for John Masefield's *Lonely Sea and Sky*?

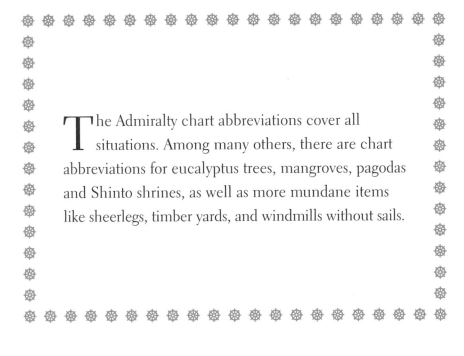

The Admiralty chart abbreviations cover all situations. Among many others, there are chart abbreviations for eucalyptus trees, mangroves, pagodas and Shinto shrines, as well as more mundane items like sheerlegs, timber yards, and windmills without sails.

Lazarette.

The usual term for the stowage compartment in the stern of a yacht.

This same name was used for the space in old sailing ships where *lazars* and other unfortunates suffering from infectious diseases were accommodated.

Admiralty charts used to show details of the early surveys in the area. Some Red Sea charts are based on original surveys carried out by ships of the *East India Company* in 1843, although there have been many revisions since. Think of the surveying crews working in open boats with sextants and leadlines in that roasting heat, and then returning to their ships where there was little comfort. And the original charts show meticulous work that originated in those stifling ships, where the day's work probably had to be completed by candle-light.

We take lighthouses for granted. Although some shore lighthouses are in inaccesible places, it was building the *rock* lighthouses that required persistence, ingenuity, skill, and sometimes bravery.

The first attempt at a light on the *Eddystone Rocks* was made 300 years ago, with the builders having to row the twelve miles out to the light. The existing light (which now has a helipad on top) was built in 1882.

'They that go down to the sea in ships
And occupy their business in great waters,
These men see the works of the Lord
And his wonders in the deep.'

PSALM 107

A yachting magazine says: '*As sails age they change shape and lose some of their efficiency.*'

Regrettably this may also apply to sailors!

Worse things happen at sea

19TH CENTURY PROVERB

'To be familiar with the knots, bends, splices, and purchases in common use at sea is an indispensable qualification for the man who would command his own little vessel. For not only must he know how to handle the various ropes connected with his rigging, belay his sheets in orthodox fashion, tie in his reef points with the proper knot, but he should be able to effect all ordinary repairs on his rigging.'

E. F. KNIGHT – *'Small Boat Sailing'*

Steer small. An old fashioned, but highly practical, expression telling the helmsman to keep as close to the ordered course as possible – perhaps in a situation where there is little room for manoeuvre.

Small stuff. The odds and ends of twine and minor cordage used for small rigging jobs.

It is fun trying to connect the names of traditional craft with the areas where they originate.

What about *Bawley*, *Dghaisa* and *Nabby*?

(Thames Estuary, Malta, and the west coast of Scotland.)

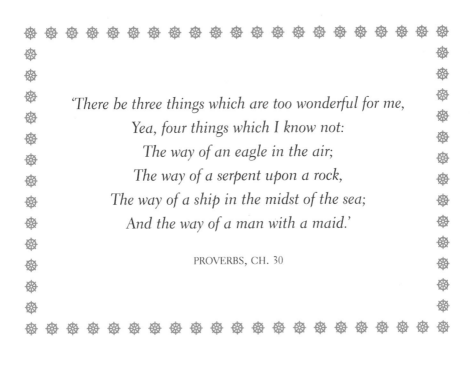

'There be three things which are too wonderful for me,
Yea, four things which I know not:
The way of an eagle in the air;
The way of a serpent upon a rock,
The way of a ship in the midst of the sea;
And the way of a man with a maid.'

PROVERBS, CH. 30

'Down dropped the breeze,
The sails dropt down
'Twas sad as sad could be
And we did speak only to break
The silence of the Sea.'

SAMUEL TAYLOR COLERIDGE –
'The Rime of the Ancient Mariner'

And the *Ancient Mariner*, poor man, had not got an engine.

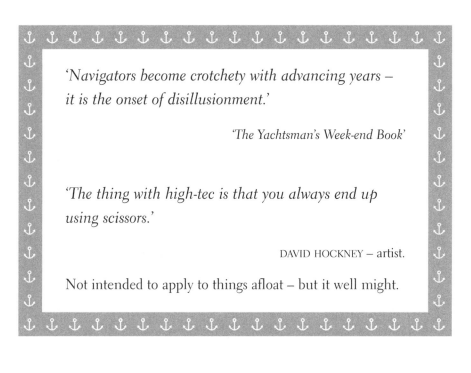

'Navigators become crotchety with advancing years –
it is the onset of disillusionment.'

'The Yachtsman's Week-end Book'

'The thing with high-tec is that you always end up
using scissors.'

DAVID HOCKNEY – artist.

Not intended to apply to things afloat – but it well might.

The Galley... *'The pan or the food that you want will always be under or behind something else that you do not want, in the deepest, farthest part of any locker – assuming you know which locker to consult in the first place.'*

JANE GIBBS – *'The Reluctant Cook'*

It seems that after the 1927 Fastnet the RORC made a rule that the rigid dinghies carried aboard (there were no inflatables then) were to be made unsinkable by having 'two 2–gallon petrol cans or buoyancy tanks of similar capacity, securely lashed in place'.

'There is of course no such thing as a perfect yacht, still less a perfect owner.'

ADLARD COLES

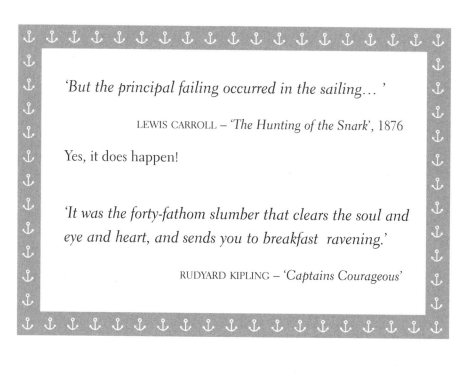

'But the principal failing occurred in the sailing… '

LEWIS CARROLL – 'The Hunting of the Snark', 1876

Yes, it does happen!

'It was the forty-fathom slumber that clears the soul and
eye and heart, and sends you to breakfast ravening.'

RUDYARD KIPLING – 'Captains Courageous'

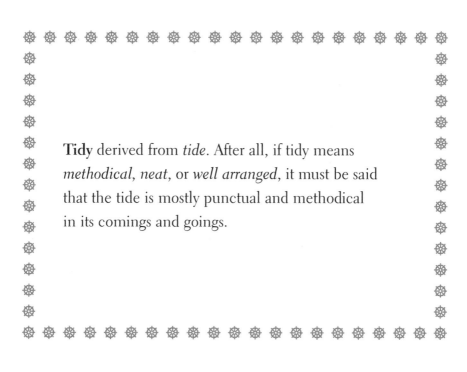

Tidy derived from *tide*. After all, if tidy means *methodical, neat,* or *well arranged,* it must be said that the tide is mostly punctual and methodical in its comings and goings.

'O Lord, when thou givest to thy servants to endeavour any great matter, grant us to know that it is not the beginning only, but the continuing of the same until it be throughly finished which yieldeth the true glory;… '

From 'Drake's Prayer'

Francis Drake's *great matter* was his 1577 global voyage in the 100 ton *Golden Hind* (rechristened after leaving England as the *Pelican*). With virtually no charts and little information about what land was where, he sailed through the Straits of Magellan into the Pacific, thence up to where San Francisco now is. He then sailed across the Pacific to the Moluccas (collecting 6 tons of cloves) and *throughly finished* his *great matter* by arriving home to Plymouth in 1580.

The dictionary defines landfall as: '*An approach to or sighting of land, esp. for the first time.*'

The most pleasing landfalls come after a long ocean passage. Although, even with a good GPS, the first sight of the Cherbourg peninsular after an overnight passage can be welcome enough. And a good moment can be on a dark night at sea when a looked for light (or its loom) is sighted just about where and when expected.

*'Experiences at sea lend themselves to
exaggeration. Strong winds become gales in the telling,
gales hurricanes, moderate seas become huge,
big waves giants.'*

FRANK MULVILLE

Especially at the yacht club bar.

D awn at sea, at least in good weather, can mean thoughts of a really good breakfast. In bad weather, it can seem easier to cope and bring hope of an improvement.

For the few who still remember wartime convoy escorts with primitive radar, dawn meant the relief in finding that your ship had not lost the convoy and you were still more or less in your right place.

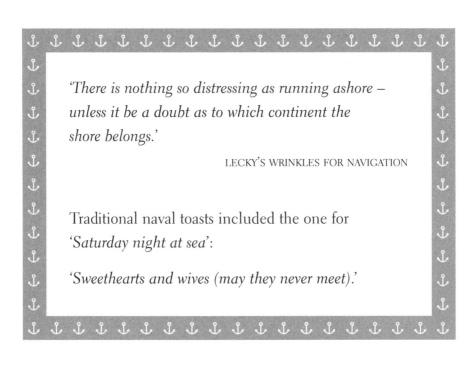

*'There is nothing so distressing as running ashore –
unless it be a doubt as to which continent the
shore belongs.'*

LECKY'S WRINKLES FOR NAVIGATION

Traditional naval toasts included the one for
'Saturday night at sea':

'Sweethearts and wives (may they never meet).'

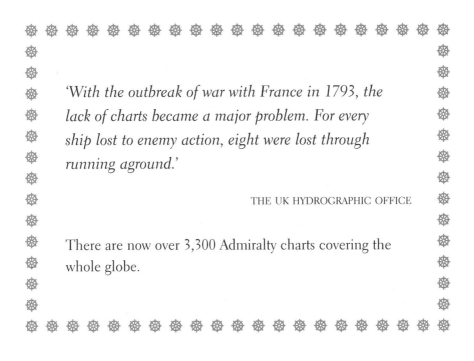

'With the outbreak of war with France in 1793, the lack of charts became a major problem. For every ship lost to enemy action, eight were lost through running aground.'

THE UK HYDROGRAPHIC OFFICE

There are now over 3,300 Admiralty charts covering the whole globe.

'To be happy for a night, get drunk;
to be happy for a month, get married;
to be happy for life, get a sailboat.'

ANON

It has been said that: *'The Master of a ship, however small she might be, has a position in life bestowed on him by his charge.'*

Sometimes known as the 'Bligh syndrome!'

A Cure for Insomnia – If You Have Ever Been a Sailor.

As you lie in bed, imagine that you are back at sea on a cold, rough night. You are in your bunk, but not sleeping well because of the noise and the motion. The boat is going to windward, so she is heeled over and you hear the odd dollop of spray landing on the deck. You know that quite soon you will be called to go on watch, and struggle into your damp clothes and oilies. Then harness on, and out into the cockpit. By this time, your own bed seems remarkably warm and attractive. And you may well just drop off to sleep.

When Tristan Jones died, the inscription on his gravestone (at his own request) was:

'Tristan Jones,
Seaman, author, and explorer
He loved life and paid his way.'

*'The majority of yachts of the Royal Yacht Club in those days
(the 1820's) carried brass cannon and an armoury of rifles
and cutlasses. The cannon were for firing salutes. As for the
cutlasses, they came in handy for cutting away rigging when
two yachts of these keen sportsman ran foul of each other…
when several thousand guineas were at stake.'*

ANTHONY HECKSTALL-SMITH – *'Sacred Cowes'*

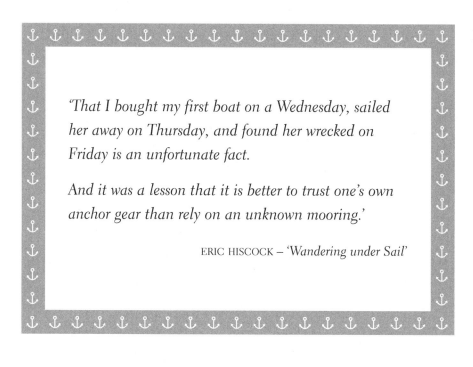

'That I bought my first boat on a Wednesday, sailed her away on Thursday, and found her wrecked on Friday is an unfortunate fact.

And it was a lesson that it is better to trust one's own anchor gear than rely on an unknown mooring.'

ERIC HISCOCK – *'Wandering under Sail'*

'Boats are like people, it isn't work that bears them quickly to the grave, but idleness. When a boat is being used she is being looked after; when she is laid up or spends week after week swinging to her mooring, she is deteriorating.'

FRANK MULALLY – 'Dear Dolphin'

'Ever since man made a dugout canoe, it has happened that, as soon as he made it big enough for two people he started having 'crew problems'.

BILL LUCAS & ANDREW SPEDDING – *'Sod's Law of the Sea'*

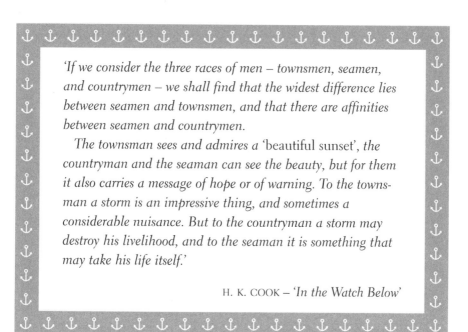

'If we consider the three races of men – townsmen, seamen, and countrymen – we shall find that the widest difference lies between seamen and townsmen, and that there are affinities between seamen and countrymen.

The townsman sees and admires a 'beautiful sunset', the countryman and the seaman can see the beauty, but for them it also carries a message of hope or of warning. To the townsman a storm is an impressive thing, and sometimes a considerable nuisance. But to the countryman a storm may destroy his livelihood, and to the seaman it is something that may take his life itself.'

H. K. COOK – 'In the Watch Below'

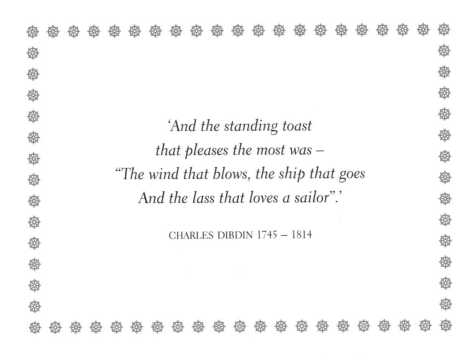

'And the standing toast
that pleases the most was –
"The wind that blows, the ship that goes
And the lass that loves a sailor".'

CHARLES DIBDIN 1745 – 1814

Beneaped. The situation where, if you were unwise enough to go aground at the top of spring tides, you would have to wait a fortnight (during which there were neap tides) before you could get off at the next spring high tide.

Getting yourself beneaped at the time of the equinox was, of course, the height of foolishness!

It is a fact that the man on the dock who says that:
'there is plenty of water over there'
never asks how much you draw.

A yachtsman's prayer.

'Dear Lord, forgive me.
I went to sea in a power boat – and I enjoyed it.'

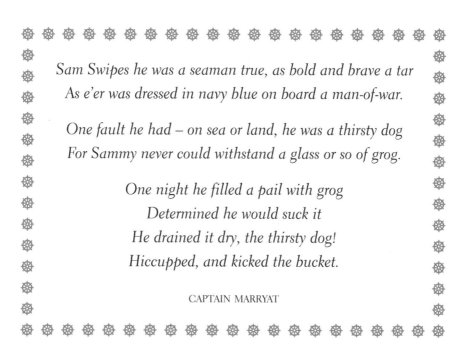

Sam Swipes he was a seaman true, as bold and brave a tar
As e'er was dressed in navy blue on board a man-of-war.

One fault he had – on sea or land, he was a thirsty dog
For Sammy never could withstand a glass or so of grog.

One night he filled a pail with grog
Determined he would suck it
He drained it dry, the thirsty dog!
Hiccupped, and kicked the bucket.

CAPTAIN MARRYAT

'Cabin arrangements are not nearly as important as the provision for the orderly stowage of gear.'

T. HARRISON BUTLER

This may be the view of a distinguished but older designer, but today it is still no use having an interior layout with several bunks and good sitting space if there is no room to stow all the gear, including personal gear, that any yacht must carry.

There is so much to look at on a chart that an innocuous looking rock or shallow patch can be easily overlooked. But anyone who cannot instantly recognise the symbols for the common dangers when he sees them on the chart, might well end up learning them the hard way.

Nowadays, when voice radio communication is taken so completely for granted, it may be hard to realise that, well within living memory, there was none.

Radio messages were sent by morse code. Ships within sight of each other used signal lamps (morse code), flags, or semaphore.

'Communicators' (they used to be called 'signalmen', 'telegraphists', or 'radio operators') needed a lot of skill.

The technical definition of navigation is:
'the art of conducting a vessel from one place to another by sea, safely, expeditiously, and efficiently'.

Which just about says it all, except that there are those who like to add: *'…and without actually hitting anything'.*

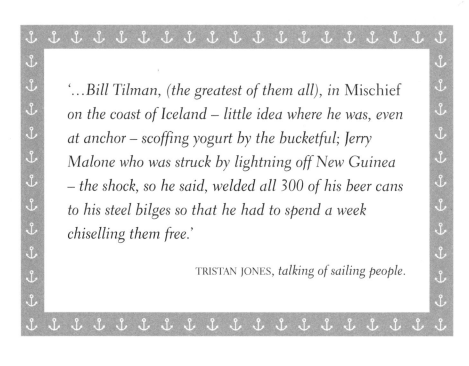

'...Bill Tilman, (the greatest of them all), in Mischief on the coast of Iceland – little idea where he was, even at anchor – scoffing yogurt by the bucketful; Jerry Malone who was struck by lightning off New Guinea – the shock, so he said, welded all 300 of his beer cans to his steel bilges so that he had to spend a week chiselling them free.'

TRISTAN JONES, *talking of sailing people.*

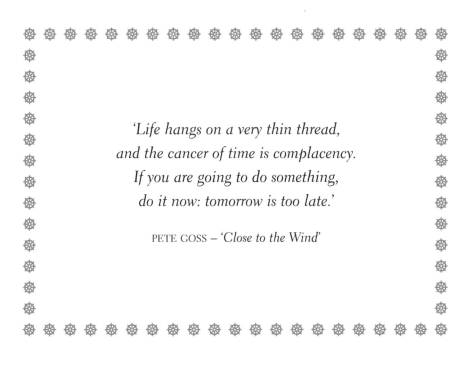

*'Life hangs on a very thin thread,
and the cancer of time is complacency.
If you are going to do something,
do it now: tomorrow is too late.'*

PETE GOSS – *'Close to the Wind'*

We take it quite for granted that our time (even though it is now officially UMT instead of GMT) and the system of longitude on all charts is based on zero degrees longitude passing through Greenwich – hence the Greenwich Meridian or Prime Meridian. In fact it passes through the courtyard of the Old Royal Observatory.

It took some time before all the countries of the world acknowledged this – some reluctantly.

The last to agree were the French in 1911.

'It is most plain, from the confusion all these people are in about how to make good their reckonings, and the disorder they are in, it is by God's Almighty Providence and great chance, that there are not a great many more misfortunes and ill chances in navigation than there are.'

SAMUEL PEPYS, commenting on naval navigation in 1683.

"'Your ship is your best lifeboat' is a saying from naval wartime experience, and the 1979 Fastnet Race demonstrated that, however uncomfortable a yacht might become in extreme weather conditions, she is the best refuge as long as she remains afloat. The liferaft should be a last resort.

Seven of the 15 fatalities on this race occurred to crew who had taken to the liferafts, and of the 24 yachts that were abandoned, 19 were recovered afloat.'

PETER BRUCE – 'Heavy Weather Sailing'

In that splendid book, *The Oxford Dictionary of Humorous Quotations,* there do not seem to be any referring to sailors or the sea. Surely sailors are not that lacking in a sense of humour – or are their more pithy quotations unrepeatable in polite society?

The dress conscious yachtsman wears a 'reefer' with the black buttons of his yacht club, while assiduously avoiding the 'blazer' with its brass buttons (at least while he is occupied with boats).

But in fact 'blazer' came into the language in the middle of the last century when the captain of HMS *Blazer* dressed his boat's crew in smart blue jackets with brass buttons, and they became known as 'The Blazers'.

An incredible number of everyday expressions have
nautical origins. But, apparently, one that does not is:
spoiling the ship for a ha'p'orth of tar.

It has been suggested that this should be:
*spoiling the "sheep"… *
and refers to applying bitumen or tar to sheep's feet.

'A solitary night watch in a sailing boat is a good time to look at the stars and think. On a balmy June night in the North Sea, while two lightships and several buoys blinked out, signalling their characteristics, as it were their signatures, I thought "when did all this begin?" Did Francis Drake have buoys to guide him as he weighed anchor in Plymouth Sound, or when he crept up to the Spanish Armada off Gravelines? And what about all those wonderful beacons and transits in the Dutch seaways and the Frisian Islands, when did all that begin? I decided to find out.'

JOHN NAISH – 'Seamarks'

Spinnaker.

Is said to have been derived from *sphinxer*, a name coined by yacht hands when it was first used aboard the yacht *Sphinx* in the Solent in the 1870's.

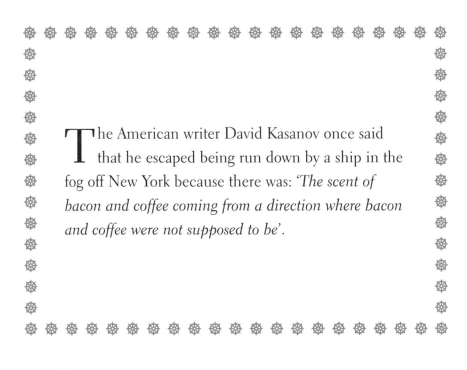

The American writer David Kasanov once said that he escaped being run down by a ship in the fog off New York because there was: *'The scent of bacon and coffee coming from a direction where bacon and coffee were not supposed to be'*.

One definition of a chart is: 'a map on which the water is of greater importance than any land which may be surrounding it'.

Charts are also described as *sailors' road maps* – which does not take account of a sailor not only needing to know where he is going, but what the depth will be when he gets there.

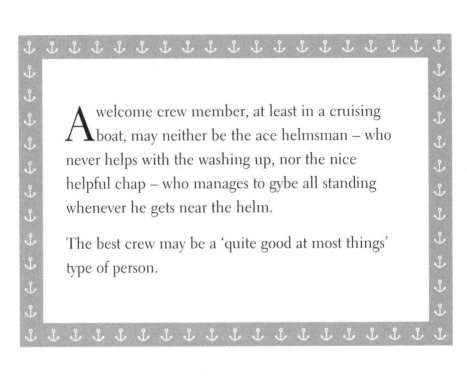

A welcome crew member, at least in a cruising boat, may neither be the ace helmsman – who never helps with the washing up, nor the nice helpful chap – who manages to gybe all standing whenever he gets near the helm.

The best crew may be a 'quite good at most things' type of person.

He might be relying on his faithful *Satnav*, but it is a rash sailor who crosses an ocean without a sextant as well.

The Royal Cork Yacht Club was founded in 1720 and claims to be the world's oldest yacht club. Somehow, despite being in the Republic of Ireland, it has never lost the *'Royal'* from its title.

A well-used Naval Prayer Book which had been used by the Captain when conducting prayers on board,
included several prayers for families. One of these contained the line:
'*And bring us back to them in thine own good time*'.

The last few words had been firmly deleted and '*soon*' pencilled in.

'As the Everest pioneer, Sir John Hunt, once remarked when he regretted the modern easy accessibility of the great mountain: "There ought to be something left in this world that keeps people humble".

There is, Cape Horn does just that'.

PETER KRIEG, round the world sailor.

Happily, most yachts never need a serious tow: that is in the open sea, not just a pluck across the harbour. But if the worst does happen, lifeboats will tell you that few crews know how to secure a tow-line properly (it may be seasickness) and often a lifeboat crewman has to be put aboard.

Perhaps this is something the wise skipper should think about.

An old East Coast bargee was watching some yachts racing and remarked: *'If I were a gen'leman, which I ain't, or rich, which I aren't, I'd never go to windward, no not never!'*

IAN DEAR, *The Royal Ocean Racing Club*

'Here lies the body of Michael O'Day
who was sunk while upholding
his Right of Way.'

ACKNOWLEDGEMENTS

Cover illustration by Martin Wiscombe, by kind permission of Handmade Designs Ltd.

Frontispiece cartoon by Mike Peyton.

Quotations by Des Sleightholme and Tom Cunliffe are reproduced by kind permission of *Yachting Monthly*.

Quotations from *Sod's Law of the Sea*, *Heavy Weather Sailing*, *The RYA Book of Navigation* and *Encounters of a Wayward Sailor* are reproduced by kind permission of Adlard Coles Nautical.

The origin of some Sayings of the Sea, both old and new, are often obscure, so due apologies are offered to anyone who has not been correctly acknowledged.